GEORGIA CHRISTOU

Georgia Christou is a writer for stage and screen.

Theatre includes *Yous Two* at Hampstead Theatre (nominated for the Verity Bargate Award and a Stage Debut Award), *How to Spot an Alien* for Paines Plough, and *Peter Pan* for Birmingham Rep (co-adapter).

Short plays include *How to Not Sink* for Sphinx Theatre (published in *Women Centre Stage* by Nick Hern Books), and *Ephrem Holmes* for DryWrite/The Bush. Georgia has taken part in the Royal Court's Young Writers Programme.

Georgia's television debut, *Through the Gates* for Channel 4, was nominated for two BAFTAs: Best Single Drama and Best Breakthrough. She has also worked on dramas for Netflix, Sky Atlantic, Channel 4 and the BBC.

Other Plays for Young People to Perform from Nick Hern Books

Original Plays

100
Christopher Heimann,
   Neil Monaghan, Diene Petterle

BANANA BOYS
Evan Placey

BLOOD AND ICE
Liz Lochhead

BOYS
Ella Hickson

BRAINSTORM
Ned Glasier, Emily Lim
   and Company Three

BUNNY
Jack Thorne

BURYING YOUR BROTHER
   IN THE PAVEMENT
Jack Thorne

COCKROACH
Sam Holcroft

DISCO PIGS
Enda Walsh

EIGHT
Ella Hickson

THE FALL
James Fritz

GIRLS LIKE THAT
Evan Placey

HOLLOWAY JONES
Evan Placey

I CAUGHT CRABS IN WALBERSWICK
Joel Horwood

MOGADISHU
Vivienne Franzmann

MOTH
Declan Greene

THE MYSTAE
Nick Whitby

OVERSPILL
Ali Taylor

PRONOUN
Evan Placey

SAME
Deborah Bruce

THE URBAN GIRL'S GUIDE TO
   CAMPING AND OTHER PLAYS
Fin Kennedy

THE WARDROBE
Sam Holcroft

Adaptations

ANIMAL FARM
Ian Wooldridge
Adapted from George Orwell

ARABIAN NIGHTS
Dominic Cooke

BEAUTY AND THE BEAST
Laurence Boswell

CORAM BOY
Helen Edmundson
Adapted from Jamila Gavin

DAVID COPPERFIELD
Alastair Cording
Adapted from Charles Dickens

GREAT EXPECTATIONS
Nick Ormerod and Declan Donnellan
Adapted from Charles Dickens

HIS DARK MATERIALS
Nicholas Wright
Adapted from Philip Pullman

THE JUNGLE BOOK
Stuart Paterson
Adapted from Rudyard Kipling

KENSUKE'S KINGDOM
Stuart Paterson
Adapted from Michael Morpurgo

KES
Lawrence Till
Adapted from Barry Hines

NOUGHTS & CROSSES
Dominic Cooke
Adapted from Malorie Blackman

THE RAILWAY CHILDREN
Mike Kenny
Adapted from E. Nesbit

SWALLOWS AND AMAZONS
Helen Edmundson and Neil Hannon
Adapted from Arthur Ransome

TO SIR, WITH LOVE
Ayub Khan-Din
Adapted from E.R Braithwaite

TREASURE ISLAND
Stuart Paterson
Adapted from Robert Louis Stevenson

WENDY & PETER PAN
Ella Hickson
Adapted from J.M. Barrie

THE WOLVES OF WILLOUGHBY
   CHASE
Russ Tunney
Adapted from Joan Aiken

Georgia Christou

BRIGHT. YOUNG. THINGS.

NICK HERN BOOKS
www.nickhernbooks.co.uk

TONIC

TONIC THEATRE
www.tonictheatre.co.uk

A Nick Hern Book

Bright. Young. Things. first published as a paperback original in Great Britain in 2020 by Nick Hern Books Limited, The Glasshouse, 49a Goldhawk Road, London W12 8QP, in association with Tonic

Bright. Young. Things. copyright © 2020 Georgia Christou

Georgia Christou has asserted her right to be identified as the author of this work

Cover image by Kathy Barber, Bullet Creative, www.bulletcreative.com

Designed and typeset by Nick Hern Books, London
Printed and bound in Great Britain by Mimeo Ltd, Huntingdon, Cambridgeshire PE29 6XX

A CIP catalogue record for this book is available from the British Library

ISBN   978 1 84842 862 1

Contents

The Platform Plays

BRIGHT. YOUNG. THINGS.
BY GEORGIA CHRISTOU

THE GLOVE THIEF
BY BETH FLINTOFF

HEAVY WEATHER
BY LIZZIE NUNNERY

THE LIGHT BURNS BLUE
BY SILVA SEMERCIYAN

RED BY SOMALIA SEATON

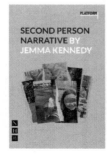

SECOND PERSON NARRATIVE
BY JEMMA KENNEDY

THIS CHANGES EVERYTHING
BY JOEL HORWOOD

PLATFORM

Commissioning and publishing a range of new plays which give girls a greater share of the action was always on my to-do list when I founded Tonic in 2011. While Tonic has very big aspirations – to support theatre in the UK to achieve greater gender equality – it is a small company and so we have to make careful choices about where we target our efforts. I spend lots of time looking to identify 'pressure points' – places where, with a bit of work, a great effect can be achieved. For this reason, much of Tonic's work focuses on partnerships with some of the largest theatres in the country, because if they change, others will follow. But it has always been clear to me that youth drama is one of the greatest pressure points of all. It is the engine room of the theatre industry; tomorrow's theatre-makers (not to mention audience members) are to be found today in youth-theatre groups, university drama societies and school drama clubs all over the country. If we can challenge their assumptions about the role of women's stories, voices, and ideas in drama, then change in the profession – in time – will be immeasurably easier to achieve.

Beyond this strategic interest in youth drama, I was convinced that girls were getting a raw deal, and I found that troubling. Having worked previously as a youth-theatre director, I was familiar with the regular challenge of trying to find scripts that had adequate numbers of female roles for all the committed and talented girls that wanted to take part. In nearly all the various youth-drama groups I worked in across a five-year period, there were significantly more girls than boys. However, when it came to finding big-cast, age-appropriate plays for them to work on, I was constantly frustrated by how few there seemed to be that provided enough opportunity for the girls. When looking at contemporary new writing for young actors to perform, one could be mistaken for thinking that youth drama was a predominantly male pursuit, rather than the other way around.

Aside from the practicalities of matching the number of roles to the number of girls in any one drama group, the nature of writing for female characters was something I struggled to get excited about. While there were some notable examples, often the writing for female characters seemed somewhat lacklustre. They tended to be characters at the periphery of the action rather than its heart, with far less to say and do than their male counterparts, and with a tendency towards being one-dimensional, rather than complex or vibrant, funny or surprising. Why was it that in the twenty-first century the *quality* as well as the *quantity* of roles being written for girls still seemed to lag behind those for boys?

Keen to check I wasn't just imagining this imbalance, Tonic conducted a nationwide research study looking into opportunities for girls in youth drama, focusing on the quantity *and* quality of roles available to them. The research was written up into a report, *Swimming in the shallow end*, and is published on the Tonic website. Not only did the research confirm my worst fears; more depressingly, it exceeded them. Many of the research participants were vocal about the social, artistic and emotional benefits that participation in youth-drama productions can have on a young person's life. But so too were they – to quote the report – on 'the erosion to self-esteem, confidence and aspiration when these opportunities are repeatedly held out of reach... [and] for too many girls, this is the case'.

But despite the doom and gloom of the research findings, there remained an exciting proposition; to write stories that weren't currently being put on stage, and to foreground – rather than ignore – the experiences, achievements and world-view of young women, perhaps the group above all others in our society whose situation has altered so dramatically and excitingly over the past hundred or so years. The brief Tonic sets Platform writers is: write a large-cast play specifically for performance by young actors, with mainly or entirely female casts and in which the female characters are no less complex or challenging than the male characters. We ask them to write in such a way that these plays can be performed by young people anywhere in the country, and that there should be scope for every school, college and youth-theatre group performing the play to make a production their own.

There are now seven Platform plays published, of which this is one, and our hope is that there will be many more. Our aspiration – fundraising permitting – is to keep commissioning titles in the series so that over time, Platform will become a new canon of writing for young actors and one that puts girls and their lives centre stage. The first three plays in the series were published in 2015 and have already been performed across the length and breadth of the United Kingdom as well as in Australia, Canada, Hong Kong, Indonesia, Ireland, Luxembourg, Malta and the USA. I look forward to hearing about productions of this play, and a future where great stories about girls and their lives are being staged in theatres, halls, drama studios and classrooms as the rule rather than the exception.

Lucy Kerbel
Director, Tonic

www.tonictheatre-platform.co.uk

Acknowledgements

Tonic would like to thank:

Matt Applewhite, Tamara von Werthern and everyone at Nick Hern Books; Dale Rooks, Poppy Marples and Chichester Festival Theatre; Jon Pashley; Moira Buffini; John and Michèle Qualtrough; the National Theatre.

Tonic acknowledges with thanks the work David Lang did in helping it with its charitable structure. His advice was always clear and practical.

TONIC

Tonic was created in 2011 to support the theatre industry to achieve greater gender equality in its workforces and repertoires. Today, Tonic partners with leading theatres and performing-arts organisations around the UK on a range of projects, schemes and creative works. Current and recent partners include the Almeida Theatre, Cast, Chichester Festival Theatre, English Touring Theatre, Headlong, Leeds Playhouse, National Theatre, New Wolsey Theatre, Northern Ballet, Royal Opera House, Royal Shakespeare Company, Sadler's Wells and Sheffield Theatres.

Tonic's approach involves getting to grips with the principles that lie beneath how our industry functions – our working methods, decision-making processes, and organisational structures – and identifying how, in their current form, these can create barriers. Once we have done that, we devise practical yet imaginative alternative approaches and work with our partners to trial and deliver them. Essentially, our goal is to equip our colleagues in UK theatre with the tools they need to ensure more talented women are given the opportunity to rise to the top.

Platform is a collaboration between Tonic and Nick Hern Books. Nick Hern Books also publishes Tonic's books: *100 Great Plays for Women* and *All Change Please: A Practical Guide to Achieving Gender Equality in Theatre*.

www.tonictheatre.co.uk

Tonic have also produced, along with UK Theatre and the Society of London Theatre (SOLT), a theatre casting toolkit to help make the UK's stages and rehearsal rooms more reflective of modern society.

www.tonictheatre.co.uk/work/toolkits-and-resources

Nick Hern Books

Theatre publishers & performing rights agents

We leapt at the chance to publish and license the Platform plays in collaboration with Tonic, and always had high hopes that by making plays available which gave young women the opportunity to take centre stage, we would improve not only their confidence levels, but also start to have a positive effect on the theatrical landscape as a whole.

After all, here at the Performing Rights Department at Nick Hern Books, we're often asked, 'Are there any plays for young people?'... 'Have you got anything for a large cast?'... and 'Is there anything with strong female roles?'

Whilst the answer to these questions is, in each case, a resounding 'Yes!' (and in fact the majority of plays we've published in recent years have been by women), the number of plays that fulfil all three of these criteria – strong roles for a large, predominantly or all-female cast of young actors – has historically been less plentiful. Yet that's where there's so much demand! Nearly every teacher and youth-theatre director in the country knows that it's girls who make up the majority of their casts, and yet the plays available are often dominated by men. Because we can generally only publish what is being produced on the professional stages of the UK, until the theatre industry starts staging more plays with these qualities, the numbers will remain low. It's a vicious circle.

Five years since the first Platform plays were published, I am delighted to report that this circle has somewhat started to disintegrate. It's a source of great pleasure that, aside from their social and political purpose, they're all excellent plays in their own right. As such, we have licensed dozens of productions of the Platform plays to date, providing opportunities and great roles to many hundreds of young women (and young men, for that matter) around the world. While this is cause for celebration, it is no reason for complacency – the journey continues – and we are delighted to publish two great new Platform plays, which will hopefully be received as enthusiastically by schools and youth-theatre groups as the five so far published in the series.

Nick Hern Books looks after the amateur performing rights to well over a thousand plays, and we know from experience that when it comes to choosing the right play it can be confusing (and pricey) to read enough of what's out there until you know which play is right for you. This is why we send out approval copies: up to three plays at a time, for thirty days, after which they have to be paid for, or returned to us in mint condition, and you just need to pay the postage. So there is no reason not to read all of the available Platform plays to see if they will suit your school, college or youth-theatre group. We're very hopeful that one of them will.

Performing rights to all seven Platform plays are available at a specially reduced rate to enable even those on a very tight budget to perform them. Discounts are also available on cast sets of scripts; and the cover images on these books can be supplied, free of charge, for you to use on your poster. If you have any questions about Platform, or any of the plays on our list, or want to talk about what you're looking for, we are always happy to speak with you. Call us on +44 (0)20 8749 4953, or email us at rights@nickhernbooks.co.uk.

And here's to many more Platform plays in the future and to all the young women (and men) bringing them to life!

Tamara von Werthern
Performing Rights Manager
Nick Hern Books

www.nickhernbooks.co.uk/plays-to-perform

Introduction
Georgia Christou

When I first talked to Lucy Kerbel about writing for Tonic's Platform series, and her reasons for commissioning the plays, she described to me a familiar scenario: that youth theatres and schools are constantly faced with a lack of plays available with enough decent roles for young female actors. Directors and teachers will be forced to overcome this in a number of ways: girls will be given one of the (often underwhelming) roles available, sometimes they might even *share* one of these roles or, to make up the numbers, they will be asked to play a man. As a young person I had been through youth theatre and, eventually, drama school myself, and having worn my fair share of sideburns I felt an instant affinity with what Lucy was describing.

So I set out to write something that would address this, but also that I might have enjoyed being in when I was at school. I wanted to play characters who were different from me (who wants to play themselves, right?), but that I recognised, in a setting that felt relevant to the world we live in.

Now, I hate reality TV. Of course when I say 'hate' what I actually mean is that I moan and roll my eyes and talk a lot about how bad it is for society, but I still tune in to every episode of anything where a celebrity will cook/ice skate/pick their nose/do nothing.

Like it or not, reality TV is so much a part of the fabric of current popular culture and so I wanted to look at it through the eyes of young people. And I settled on a branch of the reality TV machine: the competition show.

In all competition shows, the premise is that you throw together a bunch of 'ordinary' people with an exceptional talent in one area (baking/singing/I think there's a show about tattooing). They are put through a series of tests or rounds, and then the cream will rise to the top and the best person will be crowned the winner. Having been discovered as the best, the winner will go on to great fame, success and happiness and all the problems they had before the competition will melt away.

The reality, of course, is a little different, but that's for you to discuss amongst your cast. (I want to point out that I don't think competition is a bad thing. In fact, I think it's brilliant to celebrate achievement and hard work and dedication to something you love.)

In *Bright. Young. Things.*, the television show the characters are taking part in is a child-genius competition; *their* dedication happens to be to a certain type of learning. But you don't need to get too caught up in how 'smart' they are. The meaning of the play could be the same if it were about a contest in beatboxing or ice hockey. What's important is why do people want to take part in these TV shows? What are they hoping to get from the experience? And what, if anything, do they learn?

I hope this play gives you plenty to talk about. I hope you can relate to at least one of the characters. And I hope, more than anything, that you have fun creating a show together where no one has to wear sideburns. Unless of course you want to. I'll leave it with you.

Acknowledgements

To Lucy Kerbel and Tonic Theatre.

To Ben Tait and Lady Eleanor Holles School.

To Vicky Long and Neon Performing Arts.

To Jon Pashley, Poppy Marples, Megan Bewley and the team at Chichester Festival Theatre.

And to the wonderful and generous cast of young people that took part in development workshops at CFT… Thank you.

You are all just brilliant.

G.C.

Production Note

Sound

Where possible, it would be great if the sounds in the show were created live.

For example – when a contestant gets a question right, you might use a triangle. A bike horn for the 'incorrect' sound. A rainstick for rain. A drum. Whatever you can get your hands on for 'the end of the world' sequence.

There are a few places where you might also need recorded music, but they'll become apparent.

Props

There are lots of objects in this show that help tell the story. Here's a prop list to start you off:

Coffee cups
Six backpacks
A telephone
Microphones
Squeezy spray bottle
Packets of sweets and biscuits
Prawn-cocktail crisp packet
Earphones
A rabbit foot (a piece of furry material will do it!)
Two brown-paper lunch bags
A trophy
Books for revision

Staging

The staging suggestions are just that. Suggestions.

Do whatever helps you to tell the story.

BRIGHT. YOUNG. THINGS.

Characters

THE CONTESTANTS

They're written as female but I've starred the characters below that can be adapted for any gender. Please feel free to make changes to personal pronouns, etc., as necessary.

ROCHELLE
SHEARA, *Jasmine's twin*
JASMINE, *Sheara's twin*
BERNIE*
HESTER
AMBER*

THE ADULTS

All the roles below can be cast as any gender, again, please change pronouns/names, etc., as you need.

ROCHELLE'S DAD
ROCHELLE'S MUM†

PRESENTER 1
PRESENTER 2

PRODUCERS (*a minimum of three, no maximum!*)
FRANKIE
MAKE-UP ARTIST

THE JUDGES

LADY REGINA RUSTINGTON†
NEIL PULLOVER

† LADY REGINA RUSTINGTON *and* ROCHELLE'S MUM *can be doubled or be played by two actors.*

Note on Text

– at the end of a line denotes an interruption

… denotes a thought trailing off

Lines in **bold** are spoken directly to the audience

1. Everything Follows From Here

Lights up.

Either side of the stage are chairs. These are for the cast. The changes in this play should be fast, so it's going to be helpful to have your actors on hand at the drop of a hat.

On stage are six blocks arranged in a V-shape, with the pointy bit at the back.

Behind each of these blocks is a child, with a backpack next to them – AMBER, BERNIE, HESTER, JASMINE *and* SHEARA. *These are the contestants. They are all frozen, focused on something in front of them. Something we can't see.*

And on the final block is a large phone – maybe an old-fashioned one.

Behind that phone stands a man – this is ROCHELLE'S DAD. *He stares at the phone, twitchy.*

SHEARA. **Do you remember the moment just before everything changed?**

ROCHELLE, *early teens, enters.*

ROCHELLE. Dad?

JASMINE. **A door opens.**

AMBER. **A storm breaks.**

HESTER. **A phone rings.**

BERNIE. **And everything, your whole life as you now know it, follows from there.**

ROCHELLE. Dad?

ROCHELLE'S DAD. Oh hello, love.

ROCHELLE. What you doing?

ROCHELLE'S DAD. Nothing much.

ROCHELLE. I've been shouting you.

ROCHELLE'S DAD. In my own world.

ROCHELLE. You coming down for breakfast?

ROCHELLE'S DAD. Yeah.

ROCHELLE. I did eggs.

ROCHELLE'S DAD. Lovely.

ROCHELLE. We can decide what we want to do today.
Museum? Film?

Beat.

Next door have just painted their front wall. We could watch
it dry if you like?

ROCHELLE'S DAD. Sounds good.

ROCHELLE. Dad!

ROCHELLE'S DAD. What?

ROCHELLE. You're doing that thing again. That 'not listening'
thing.

ROCHELLE'S DAD. Sorry, love.

ROCHELLE. Your eggs are getting cold.

ROCHELLE'S DAD. Yes. Right.

The PRODUCERS *enter, holding a mobile phone.*

(*A word on the* PRODUCERS: *they should feel – breathe,
move – like one person, even if there's twenty of them. They are
strange and slightly other-worldly. Their props could be
oversized or they might wear bits of the same costume – like
different components of a matching suit. Shirt, tie, jacket, etc.
You can split their lines as you see fit – they can speak
separately or together or a mixture of both. It might help to
think of them as a single, many-headed beast.*)

ROCHELLE. You know staring at it won't make it ring.

Then the sound of a phone ringing. It's not in ROCHELLE's *world.* ROCHELLE *and her* DAD *freeze.*

JASMINE, SHEARA, AMBER, HESTER *and* BERNIE *all answer their phones.*

JASMINE, SHEARA, AMBER, HESTER *and* BERNIE. Hello?

PRODUCERS. It's the producers calling.

From the studio.

We're phoning with the result of your application.

A light drum rolls.

We were overwhelmed by this year's applicants.

The competition was very tough.

I'm afraid it's not good news...

The drum stops.

Beat.

It's great news!

You made the show. Congratulations.

The CONTESTANTS *celebrate, punch the air. Squeal with happiness. The actors at the side of the stage cheer too!*

At the same time FRANKIE *enters with a cup of coffee.*

FRANKIE *hands the* PRODUCERS *the cup (or cups – maybe she hands one to each of them). The cup(s) get dropped with a clatter.*

PRODUCERS. DRAT!

Everyone stops cheering.

Oh. I wasn't talking to you.

Everyone makes a loud sigh of relief.

FRANKIE *scrabbles around, picking up cups.*

Be at the studio for eleven. And remember this moment. Everything you've ever wanted...

JASMINE, SHEARA, AMBER, HESTER *and* BERNIE.
Everything?

ALL PRODUCERS. Everything follows from here.

The line goes dead.

The CHILDREN *pick up their backpacks and turn upstage.*

All except ROCHELLE *and her* DAD – *who keep staring at the phone.*

ROCHELLE. Come on, Dad.

Her DAD *turns and walks away.*

The phone rings.

ROCHELLE'S DAD *grabs it.*

ROCHELLE'S DAD. Elaine?

PRODUCERS. Not the last time I checked.

ROCHELLE'S DAD. Oh. Sorry, boss. I thought you were someone else.

PRODUCERS. We need you to come in today.

ROCHELLE'S DAD. Today?

PRODUCERS. We wouldn't ask but it's urgent.

ROCHELLE'S DAD. As in *today*, today?

PRODUCERS. Is there a problem?

ROCHELLE'S DAD. No.

PRODUCERS. Good. Then I'll see you –

ROCHELLE'S DAD. Actually, yes. My daughter. We were supposed to be spending the day together.

PRODUCERS. We totally understand.

ROCHELLE'S DAD. You do?

PRODUCERS. Absolutely.

ROCHELLE'S DAD. I really appreciate it.

PRODUCERS. It will be no trouble, just bring her with you.

ROCHELLE'S DAD (*disappointed*). Bring her...

PRODUCERS. No need to thank us.

ROCHELLE'S DAD. Right. Yes. Thank you, I'll see you.

The line goes dead.

(*To* ROCHELLE.) Change of plan.

Theme music plays.

The PRODUCERS *exit and at the same time two people enter. They're holding microphones. These are the* PRESENTERS.

2. The Presenters

PRESENTER 1. I'm going to throw a word into the room and I want everyone to think about what it means to them. Okay?

PRESENTER 2. Okay.

PRESENTER 1. AJ, are we ready?

PRESENTER 2. I'm ready, SJ.

PRESENTER 1. Studio audience, are you ready?

Silence.

Then here we go...

Beat.

'Genius.'

A MAKE-UP ARTIST *enters and touches up their faces as they speak.*

PRESENTER 2. You just threw it out there.

PRESENTER 1. Dropped the G-bomb.

PRESENTER 2 (*like a bomb going off*). Kapoooow.

Throughout the remainder of the scene, various people come and go – they might change one of their jackets, bring on a new pair of shoes, hairspray… you get the picture.

The PRESENTERS, *meanwhile, can act as if all these minions aren't there and plough on through their script regardless.*

PRESENTER 1. A small word.

PRESENTER 2. With a big meaning.

PRESENTER 1. It is inspiration.

PRESENTER 2. Aspiration.

PRESENTER 1. Unlimited potential.

PRESENTER 2. Twelve months ago, we began a search.

PRESENTER 1. In libraries and schools.

PRESENTER 2. Cities and suburbs.

PRESENTER 1. No stone was left unturned in our search to find Britain's brightest child. Thousands applied. And after a tough elimination process –

PRESENTER 2. We've whittled it down to just six. Now our brainy babes –

A voice from the dark speaks.

PRODUCERS. I don't like that.

PRESENTER 2. The jacket?

PRODUCERS. The line. It's tacky.

PRESENTER 2. It was in the script.

PRODUCERS. Any suggestions?

   'Unique youngsters'?

   'Clued-up kids'?

   Try it.

PRESENTER 2. Our clued-up kids –

PRODUCERS. Better!

PRESENTER 2. Will be flexing their thinkers in five gruelling intelligence tests:

PRESENTER 1. Maths.

PRESENTER 2. Spelling.

PRESENTER 1. Memory.

PRESENTER 2. General knowledge.

PRESENTER 1. And the final round – the head-to-head.

PRESENTER 2. But with a contestant leaving the competition in every round, only one child can come out on top in the fight –

PRODUCERS. Try 'battle'.

PRESENTER 2. In the battle to lift the coveted 'Golden Brain' and be crowned this year's –

BOTH PRESENTERS. BRIGHT YOUNG THING!

PRODUCERS. And then that'll be your cue to step forward.

The CONTESTANTS *all turn around to face the audience.*

Don't be shy.

They step forward in a line.

The audience will clap.

The PRODUCERS *start clapping and turn to invite the audience to do the same.*

Then one by one you're going to introduce yourselves. Look straight into the camera and…

FRANKIE *enters, followed by* ROCHELLE *and her* DAD.

FRANKIE. Boss?

PRODUCERS. What is it, Frankie?

FRANKIE. Mr Taylor's here.

PRODUCERS. Ah yes. Thanks for coming in at such short notice.

ROCHELLE'S DAD. You said there was an emergency?

PRODUCERS. There's been a spillage.

ROCHELLE'S DAD. Okay?

PRODUCERS. I need someone to clear it up.

ROCHELLE'S DAD. Right.

PRODUCERS. And I think you might be that someone.

Beat.

ROCHELLE. They called you all the way here for that?

ROCHELLE'S DAD. Rochelle! (*To the* PRODUCERS.) I'll
   sort it.

PRODUCERS. Good. Where were we?

   ROCHELLE *and her* DAD *exit.*

   Ah yes. Introductions.

3. Introductions

*Through this scene it would be helpful if you could get a sense
of focus on each child as they speak – maybe each kid stands on
a box when it's their turn. Maybe there's a spotlight that they
step into. Or a sound. I'll use a bell sound – but go for anything
that helps.*

A bell rings.

First up:

BERNIE. Is it me? Right. I'm Bernadette. Or Bernie, if you can
   tolerate abbreviations. I'm thirteen, I like West End musicals,
   long walks and –

PRODUCERS. I'm going to pause you there.

   Could you read off the autocue?

BERNIE. Auto-what?

PRODUCERS. Just there. You see that script?

BERNIE looks out to the audience.

BERNIE. Yes.

PRODUCERS. Stick to that.

BERNIE. Right?

PRODUCERS. Go ahead.

BERNIE. I'm Bernadette. Also known as The Brain.

PRODUCERS. Carry on.

BERNIE. The others better watch out. Cos when it comes to numbers, I'm your one.

The bell rings again.

HESTER. Hester Hawthorne. Twelve years old. St Bartholomew's for Girls. Highly confident. Highly focused. Highly prepared.

The bell rings.

Next are JASMINE *and* SHEARA. *They should be dressed identically. That's important for later. They too read the autocue.*

JASMINE. She's Sheara.

SHEARA. And she's Jasmine.

JASMINE *and* SHEARA. And together we're the Dealey twins.

JASMINE. We really don't mind who wins today.

Beat.

SHEARA *and* JASMINE. So long as it's one of us.

The bell rings.

Next is AMBER. *She's wearing a large pair of headphones.*

AMBER (*too loud*). Is it me?

PRODUCERS. You might want to remove your earphones.

AMBER. I can't hear you.

PRODUCERS. You can go anyway.

AMBER (*still too loud*). I'm gonna go anyway. I'm Amber. I'm nearly ten. I'm hungry.

PRODUCERS. We'll edit that later.

The bell rings.

Everyone looks to the final box. It's empty.

We're missing one.

One?

A child, I'm counting five.

One, two, three, four, five.

There should be six.

FRANKIE. Six?

PRODUCERS. Six.

FRANKIE. I'll get on it.

The PRODUCERS *watch* FRANKIE *as she crosses to exit.*

PRODUCERS. Now!

All the PRODUCERS *clap their hands together once.*

If you're wondering what we've done with your parents –

We've locked them up.

Joking.

The PRODUCERS *all laugh.*

Actually, not joking.

They all stop laughing.

All guardians have been detained in a holding room.

We've found their presence can be a little distracting.

FRANKIE *re-enters.*

Well?

FRANKIE. Yes fine, thank you. You?

PRODUCERS. I don't mean are you well. I mean well, where is he?

FRANKIE. Who?

PRODUCERS. The final contestant.

FRANKIE. Oh. He's not coming.

Downstage we cut into ROCHELLE*'s conversation with her* DAD. *He's got a squeezy bottle and is scrubbing at the floor.*

ROCHELLE'S DAD. It's not working, Roch.

ROCHELLE. Give it here.

He hands her the bottle.

We go back to the PRODUCERS*' conversation.*

PRODUCERS. What do you mean he's not coming?

FRANKIE. His mum just called.

The PRODUCERS *breathe deeply together, like they're hyperventilating.*

Stomach flu.

They take another breath.

Quite violent apparently, all up the walls.

Breath.

She said she put it in an email?

PRODUCERS. We don't read emails.

We pay you to read emails.

This is a disaster.

The whole show, all the set-ups,

Lighting,

Shots are created around there being six children.

We must have a back-up?

FRANKIE. You didn't want to pay the train fare.

PRODUCERS. Then we're done for.

Finished.

Cancelled.

FRANKIE. It's not that bad, is it?

PRODUCERS. Where on earth are we going to find a child with an ethereal charm and a minimum IQ of one hundred and sixty?

Downstage ROCHELLE *hands her* DAD *a different squeezy bottle.*

ROCHELLE. Try this. The H_2O_2 in the sodium percarbonate will work as an oxidising agent.

ROCHELLE'S DAD. What?

ROCHELLE. Here. Out the way.

She takes the squeezy bottle.

The PRODUCERS *close in, in a semi-circle around her.*

ROCHELLE *looks up.*

ROCHELLE (*staged whisper*). Sorry!

Beat.

What?

4. Will She or Won't She?

ROCHELLE *and her* DAD *are still downstage. The* PRODUCERS *stand in a huddle behind them.*

ROCHELLE. I dunno.

ROCHELLE'S DAD. Why not?

ROCHELLE. I thought we were going cinema?

ROCHELLE'S DAD. It's an opportunity, this. Once in a lifetime.

ROCHELLE. An opportunity to embarrass myself.

ROCHELLE'S DAD. They're my bosses, Rochelle.

The PRODUCERS *lean in to listen.*

ROCHELLE. They're weird.

ROCHELLE *turns to look at them. The* PRODUCERS *pretend not to listen.*

Besides, I'm not a child genius.

ROCHELLE'S DAD. You got a scholarship to that fancy school.

ROCHELLE. This is different. These kids are super brains. Have you even seen the show?

ROCHELLE'S DAD. Course. Watched it with your mum.

Beat.

She loves all these.

ROCHELLE. Dad…

ROCHELLE'S DAD. You're right. Stupid idea.

ROCHELLE. You want me to tell them?

ROCHELLE'S DAD. No. Leave it with me.

He approaches the PRODUCERS.

PRODUCERS. Well?

ROCHELLE'S DAD. I've spoken with my daughter. Unfortunately –

ROCHELLE. I'll do it!

Beat.

ROCHELLE'S DAD. You will?

PRODUCERS. She will!

ROCHELLE *goes and stands behind the empty block.*

Good. Now that's settled.

We'd like to leave you with two questions.

The most important questions that you'll hear all day.

The CONTESTANTS *lean in.*

What does this competition mean to you?

ALL CONTESTANTS. It means everything.

PRODUCERS. What would you do to win it?

ALL CONTESTANTS. I'll do anything.

All the adults leave. The CONTESTANTS *are left alone.*

They each settle at a block.

5. Egg Sandwich Mixed with Perfume

JASMINE. Well, you've had a turn-up for the books.

ROCHELLE. Me?

JASMINE. A written application, two interviews and a screen test. And she rode in on a bottle of bleach.

SHEARA. Jasmine!

JASMINE. I just hope there's no special treatment. Given her dad works for the company.

SHEARA. Sorry about my sister. She's actually nicer than she's letting on.

ROCHELLE. It's fine.

Across the room, AMBER – *still wearing her headphones – starts humming to herself along with the music.*

She unpacks her bag. She pulls out huge packets of biscuits and sweets.

SHEARA. You brought snacks, good idea.

AMBER *doesn't answer, engrossed in what she's doing.*

You like sweet things, then?

ROCHELLE. I don't think she can hear you?

SHEARA *taps* AMBER *on the shoulder.*

AMBER *takes her headphones off to speak.*

AMBER. I didn't do anything!

SHEARA. Oh, sorry I didn't mean to scare you.

AMBER. Don't tell my nan, okay?

SHEARA. Okay?

AMBER. She'll flip her lid if she finds out.

JASMINE. Finds out what?

AMBER. My supply. She said no treats cos I didn't practise my piece last night.

HESTER. Of course. *Amber…*

AMBER. Yeah?

HESTER. I thought I recognised you. I couldn't place you without the violin. It's me, Hester.

Beat.

We met before.

Beat. AMBER *looks blank.*

Backstage. Royal Albert Hall. My aunt curated the evening you were a part of.

JASMINE. Am I missing something?

HESTER. Amber Appleby. As in *the* Amber Appleby. I saw her play a concerto. Tchaikovsky. My dad and I go to the Proms every year, family tradition.

AMBER. Oh, that.

HESTER. It was a superb evening, wasn't it?

AMBER. I got a light-up stick which Nan said was a waste of money. Then she did a really loud fart on the coach home.

HESTER. What was it like, though?

AMBER. Sort of egg sandwich mixed with perfume.

HESTER. I meant the show. Being up there in front of all those
people?

AMBER. I don't remember much. I never do when I'm playing.
Nan said the Queen looked happy though.

AMBER puts her headphones back on.

HESTER. Crikey.

Elsewhere, BERNIE *approaches the* TWINS.

BERNIE. I saw a video of conjoined twin alligators once. They
shared a nervous system but despite this – one would bite the
other, therefore inflicting pain on himself. Fascinating stuff.
I'm Bernie.

SHEARA. That's Jasmine. I'm Sheara.

BERNIE (*genuine*). Do you have to dress the same?

JASMINE. We've worn the same outfit every day since the day
we were born.

SHEARA. Our parents started it.

JASMINE. But we'd do it anyway. We do everything the same.
Same subjects. Same meals.

SHEARA. Same socks.

BERNIE. And you don't mind?

JASMINE. Why would we?

BERNIE. I didn't mean to cause offence.

JASMINE (*light/genuine*). Oh don't worry. We're really not
here to make friends.

BERNIE. Right. No. Me neither.

BERNIE *looks disappointed. That most definitely* is *why
she's here.*

ROCHELLE. Which is your favourite, Bernie?

BERNIE. What?

ROCHELLE. Musical. You said earlier.

BERNIE. Are you actually asking? Or are you collecting ammunition against me?

ROCHELLE. Actually asking.

BERNIE. Right. Can't be too careful.

Beat.

I love them all. The singing. The dancing – the way everyone moves together, in perfect unison. I've always thought it captures a feeling. What it must feel like to really be *part* of something.

ROCHELLE. Yeah?

BERNIE. On my first day at university I'd hoped everyone might jump up on their desks and break into song like they do in the films. But they just ate out of Tupperware and talked about their hangovers.

SHEARA. You're at university?

BERNIE. No.

Beat.

Not any more. I graduated last year. How about you?

ROCHELLE. I'm not quite at uni level yet.

BERNIE. Maybe not. But I couldn't help overhearing your dad say you got a school scholarship.

ROCHELLE. Oh. Yeah. It was a boarding school. I didn't take it.

BERNIE. Why not?

A voice from offstage –

FRANKIE (*offstage*). Bernadette to the podium, please. Bernadette to the podium.

BERNIE. Looks like I'm up first.

ROCHELLE. Bernie. Good luck.

6. Round One – Mathematics

PRESENTER 1. It's finally here.

PRESENTER 2. The moment we've all been waiting for.

PRESENTER 1. We have two very special guests adjudicating the competition today.

PRESENTER 2. From British MENSA – she's fierce, she's formidable – it's Lady Regina Rustington.

PRESENTER 1. And – from *Cats Do the Funniest Things* – it's Neil Pullover.

The JUDGES *enter.*

PRESENTER 2. Lady Rustington. Any advice for our contestants when they're up on the podium today?

REGINA RUSTINGTON. Don't look down.

PRESENTER 1. Great advice from Lady Rustington. How about you Neil. Seen any good cat videos lately?

NEIL PULLOVER. I'll tell you, SJ. Or is it AJ? I can never tell these two apart.

The sound of a comedy drum sting. Ba-dum – tshhh.

Seeing as you asked, I watched one just this morning. An American Bobtail on a jet ski. It was so funny it hurt me – ow!

That drum again. Ba-dum – tshhh.

PRESENTER 2. Thank you, Neil.

PRESENTER 1. I love it when he says that.

PRESENTER 2. First to the podium is... Bernadette!

BERNIE *stands on the podium.*

(A word on the podium: you can set it wherever you want. It could be a permanent fixture downstage. It could be upstage in the middle of the V of blocks. It could be that you establish a language where a child can climb on top of any one of the blocks that's already set and that becomes the podium. In the

world of the play it's on stage, in front of a studio audience.
It's where the kids go to compete and so should feel separate
to the backstage area.)

PRESENTER 1. Bernie. You'll have one minute to answer as
many questions as you can. Your time starts... now.

REGINA RUSTINGTON. What is five thousand, four hundred
and six divided by three?

BERNIE. One thousand, eight hundred and two.

The ding of a triangle.

NEIL PULLOVER. Correct. If 3x plus 4 is equal to the value of
2x plus 6, then what is the value of 'x'?

BERNIE. Two.

The ding of a triangle.

REGINA RUSTINGTON. What is the square root of eight
thousand, four hundred and sixty-four?

BERNIE *addresses the audience.*

BERNIE. **Here's the thing about maths. You know where
you stand. There's a right answer and it doesn't matter
how you say it, or if you make the correct kind of eye
contact or what trainers you're wearing. You'll still have
got it right.**

REGINA RUSTINGTON. Bernadette?

BERNIE. **I could get it wrong, I suppose?**

NEIL PULLOVER. Is she okay?

BERNIE (*to* REGINA RUSTINGTON). The answer is
ninety-two.

Ding.

REGINA RUSTINGTON. Correct.

BERNIE. **Equations are easy. I wish there was an equation
for people.**

7. Nelson's Foot

About ten minutes later.

HESTER *is standing frozen centre stage. Her arms and legs are stretched wide, mouth open like a silent screaming statue.*

SHEARA *enters.*

JASMINE. Sheara!

SHEARA (*pointing to* HESTER – *who's still frozen*). Is she okay?

JASMINE. How was it?

HESTER. Shhhhh.

BERNIE. She's power-posing.

SHEARA. Power what?

    HESTER *finally runs out of breath. She relaxes, gasping.*

HESTER. Posing. It's a self-confidence technique. You see how I stand taller? How intimidating I look? The external affects the internal.

BERNIE. Fascinating.

JASMINE. That's one word for it.

HESTER. You can't deny the proof, Jasmine. Nine points in the first round, not too shabby if I do say so myself.

JASMINE. Which you do.

HESTER. Of course the first round is the easiest. It's endurance that's the measure of any performance. You should know that I once ran a half marathon. In the desert. Without any water.

    SHEARA *slumps onto a chair.*

JASMINE. Don't listen to her. What did you get?

    Everyone gathers around her.

SHEARA. Six.

    This settles in the room, everyone adding up what that means for them.

JASMINE. That's great.

SHEARA. What did everyone else get?

Everyone looks awkward.

JASMINE. Nine for me and Hester. Eleven for Bernie.

SHEARA. Well, that's it for me then.

HESTER. What do you mean?

SHEARA. I mean I'm gonna be first to leave.

JASMINE. Maths is your weak spot. If we can get through this then we'll win the thing. Plus Rochelle and Amber are still to go. You'll beat them easy.

HESTER. At times like this I recall the family motto. Never retreat, never surrender!

BERNIE. At the end of the day it's down to luck, isn't it.

Beat.

HESTER. No.

JASMINE. Absolutely not.

BERNIE. There's a degree of chance to everything. Like the order we went in. Sheara, you might have known the answer to all of my questions.

HESTER. I.M.H.O. –

JASMINE. Oh god.

HESTER. There's a good chance what you're suffering from is performance anxiety. Would you be interested in learning a power pose?

BERNIE. I'm not sure now's quite the right moment.

HESTER. It's about being able to deliver. It's one thing being bright when you're alone in your room. It's quite another when you're out there, in front of the crowds. That's why my sporting background puts me at an advantage.

BERNIE. What sport do you play, Hester?

HESTER. Oh you know. Rugby, hockey, rowing. The usual stuff.

JASMINE. You didn't score as high as Bernie. She's not sporty.

BERNIE. That's rather an assumption.

JASMINE. What?

BERNIE. Because I like to kick back with a quadratic equation, I can't also be captain of the football team?

SHEARA. Are you?

BERNIE. What?

SHEARA. Captain of the football team?

BERNIE. No. But that's not the point.

ROCHELLE enters.

Everyone turns to look at her. You could cut the tension with a knife.

HESTER. Rochelle!

SHEARA. What did you get? Actually don't tell me. Actually *do* tell me. I *knew* I'd be first out.

JASMINE. Let her speak.

Beat.

ROCHELLE. Three.

Beat.

SHEARA. Three?

JASMINE (*to* SHEARA). What did I tell you?

HESTER (*to* ROCHELLE). Good effort, old thing.

BERNIE. Yes, good job.

SHEARA. I only got a six and I've been practising months.

ROCHELLE (*genuine*). That's great. You won't be first out.

SHEARA. I didn't mean to…

ROCHELLE. It's fine. I *should* be first to go. It's only fair.

JASMINE. There's still Amber to go.

SHEARA. I hope she's getting on okay.

HESTER. Why wouldn't she be?

SHEARA. She's just so... young.

JASMINE. We're all young, Shear. That's sort of the point.

BERNIE. Well, she can certainly pack away those biscuits. She ate at least six before she went on.

ROCHELLE. I counted eight.

HESTER. We just need to be kind and supportive. Kindness costs nothing after all.

JASMINE. But if it did cost something, I'm sure you could afford it.

HESTER. Sorry?

JASMINE. Your dad probably owns a helicopter or something.

HESTER. He does not.

Beat.

We borrow my aunt's every now again but –

Suddenly SHEARA *SCREAMS!*

SHEARA. Argh!

JASMINE. What? What is it?

SHEARA. What is *that*?

She points at the ground.

ROCHELLE, SHEARA, BERNIE *and* JASMINE *crowd around the... thing.*

JASMINE. It looks like a mouse?

SHEARA. A dead mouse.

HESTER *joins them.*

HESTER. Panic over. My apologies. That's Nelson's foot.

JASMINE. What?

HESTER. Nelson was my rabbit. And that's his foot.

SHEARA picks it up.

SHEARA. You carry your dead rabbit's foot around?

HESTER. It's lucky.

JASMINE. If that was true it wouldn't be dead.

SHEARA. Here, Bernie. Catch!

She throws it and BERNIE catches.

HESTER is trying to be casual about this but is struggling.

HESTER. Ha. Okay, well give it here.

The others are passing it between them. It becomes like a game of piggy in the middle.

JASMINE. Thought you didn't believe in luck?

HESTER. It's not a big deal.

JASMINE. Let's see.

HESTER. Just give it BACK!

Beat.

Please.

ROCHELLE *takes it and gives it back to* HESTER.

FRANKIE *enters with* AMBER.

FRANKIE. There we go. You take a seat.

JASMINE. You alright, Amber?

FRANKIE. She'll be fine.

ROCHELLE. What happened?

FRANKIE. I think the nerves got the better of you, eh?

SHEARA (*quietly to* JASMINE). Told you.

HESTER. We *had* wondered how you'd cope.

JASMINE. Do you want to talk about it?

SHEARA. Of course she doesn't. Even if you didn't score *any* points, Amber, then it doesn't matter. You've done brilliantly to get here.

AMBER. I did.

SHEARA. Then that's great.

HESTER. What did you get? Out of interest?

AMBER. Ten.

Beat.

And then I threw up.

8. Goodbye Amber

PRESENTER 2. Well, it's been an explosive first round, hasn't it, SJ?

PRESENTER 1. It sure has.

PRESENTER 1 *wipes his shoes with a flannel.*

PRESENTER 2. And despite scoring a whopping ten points, Amber is the first one to leave the competition on medical grounds.

PRESENTER 2. She's got guts, eh SJ?

PRESENTER 1. Yeah. I'm covered in them.

PRESENTER 2. Here's us wishing Amber a speedy recovery. And while SJ's wiping her breakfast off his shoes, let's get back to the competition for Round Two. The Memory Test.

9. Round Two – Memory Test

The CONTESTANTS *are all bent low over pieces of paper.*
Quiet. Concentrated.

HESTER *looks up from behind her piece of paper and talks to*
the audience.

HESTER. **A memory. I'm in Year 4. And Dad comes to pick**
me up from school. He tells me Granny's in hospital. I
don't know much about hospital. But I do know my dad.
And his face is saying – this is bad news.

That night I made a deal with myself. If I ate all my
vegetables, then Granny would feel a bit better. If I did my
homework extra fast, then she would be able to sit up in
her bed. If I didn't touch the bottom step on the landing
then she would be able to walk about again. I did this
every day. And a week later, Granny came out of hospital.

Since then I make deals like that all the time. That if I get
an 'A' no one will get sick. If I win the hundred metres
the ice caps won't melt. Earthquakes, global warming…
as long as I don't give up, nothing bad will happen. As
long as I don't give up.

SHEARA *suddenly BANGS her fists on the table.*

SHEARA. This is impossible!

JASMINE. Shhhhh.

SHEARA. There's no logic, no pattern, they may as well have
given us a random list of words to memorise.

ROCHELLE. I suppose that's the point.

SHEARA (*to* BERNIE). Why aren't you looking at your map?

BERNIE. I am.

SHEARA. No you're not. You're reading a book. Look!

It's true. BERNIE *is hiding a book under her desk.*

SHEARA *grabs it, reads the cover.*

'*So You Want to Be on Broadway? An Idiot's Guide to*
Becoming a Star.'

BERNIE. I… I needed a break.

JASMINE. We've got half an hour to memorise every road in central Paris. And you're brushing up on your Andrew Lloyd Webber.

ROCHELLE. She doesn't need to revise.

BERNIE. Of course I do.

ROCHELLE. But you've got a photographic memory, right?

BERNIE *doesn't answer.*

SHEARA. A photographic memory?

HESTER. Personally I find that hard to believe.

JASMINE. Why?

HESTER. No disrespect, old chap. It's just become one of those things everyone *says* they have, but very few people actually do.

ROCHELLE. Like 'a good sense of humour'.

HESTER. Exactly.

JASMINE. Okay. You've got ten seconds.

JASMINE *gets a crisp packet and holds it up in front of* BERNIE.

She takes it away.

Now. Tell me the list of ingredients.

BERNIE. I… I can't.

HESTER. Case in point.

JASMINE. Try at least.

Beat.

Suit yourself.

BERNIE (*she speaks fast but is almost weary*). Potatoes, sunflower oil, sugar, glucose, salt, citric acid, potassium chloride, dried yeast, tomato extract and sweetener – open bracket, sucralose, close bracket.

Beat.

It's not something I'm proud of.

HESTER. That's...

JASMINE. Sick!

BERNIE (*to* ROCHELLE). How did you know?

ROCHELLE. My mum's the same.

SHEARA. So does that mean, you've learnt the whole map?

BERNIE. Not learnt as such.

SHEARA. But you can see it in your mind?

BERNIE. Yes.

SHEARA. Great. I've literally got no hope.

JASMINE. She's got a point.

SHEARA. Thanks!

JASMINE. No, I mean for the rest of us. We might as well give up now.

BERNIE. Please don't say that.

JASMINE. You have to admit it puts you at an advantage.

BERNIE. I could test you?

SHEARA. No. Thanks.

The others go back to their revision, all apart from BERNIE *and* ROCHELLE.

BERNIE (*to* ROCHELLE). Do you know where the word 'prodigy' comes from?

ROCHELLE. What?

BERNIE. The Latin. Prodigium. 'A monster that violates the natural order.'

ROCHELLE (*struggling to understand*). Okay?

BERNIE. You shouldn't have told them. About my memory.

ROCHELLE. It's nothing to be ashamed of.

BERNIE. No?

ROCHELLE. You're lucky. Some people would do anything to be like you. To have a kid like you.

BERNIE. Now it's like being back at school. People don't like it when things come easier to you. They don't like being around someone who makes them feel stupid. They don't like… me.

BERNIE *exits*.

Beat.

HESTER. Should someone go after her?

ROCHELLE. I didn't realise.

HESTER. Of course you didn't.

JASMINE. None of us did. But right now we've got a map to memorise. Rochelle, I don't think beating yourself up is going to help Bernie in any way.

ROCHELLE. No.

Beat.

But I think I know something that might.

They all huddle round ROCHELLE.

Then they split up and hide – one behind each block.

10. Part of Something

The holding room, moments later. BERNIE *enters.*

She looks around – everyone's gone.

Then SHEARA *pops up from behind a block.*

BERNIE. Sheara?

SHEARA *doesn't say anything. But she does move.*

Stamp, stamp, clap.

Stamp, stamp, clap.

She keeps doing it through –

What are you…

Now HESTER *has also popped up from behind a block. She joins in, in the same rhythm:*

Stamp, stamp, clap.

ROCHELLE *and* JASMINE *pop up at the same time. Stamp, stamp, clap. Maybe all the offstage characters join in too. To give it some real power.*

SHEARA (*over the noise*). We're sorry, Bernie.

HESTER. Will you forgive us?

BERNIE. What is this?

BERNIE *is centre stage, facing upstage. She holds her hand up and the stamping STOPS.*

BERNIE *turns to face the audience – a penny has dropped.*

Then MUSIC – Queen's 'We Will Rock You' – starts at the point that Freddie Mercury's voice kicks in (around eleven seconds in). Maybe it's real? Maybe it's in their heads. But it should be LOUD.

They perform a dance – that's for you to create. It needn't be complicated or anything like a musical. In fact they shouldn't be brilliant dancers.

What matters is two things: there's a point where they're all doing the same thing at the same time. In perfect unison. And BERNIE *is right in the heart of it all.*

FRANKIE *enters – taking in the scene. A scene that looks like togetherness.*

FRANKIE. What is going on in here?

The music stops. The CONTESTANTS *freeze, like animals in a headlight.*

Bernadette. Are you ready?

BERNIE *picks up her bag*.

JASMINE. Bernie? Where are you going?

SHEARA. Is she in trouble?

HESTER. If you're taking her, you'll have to take us all.

FRANKIE. Didn't she tell you? She quit.

ROCHELLE. This is my fault.

JASMINE. Can't she change her mind?

SHEARA. You can't just leave, Bernie.

BERNIE. It's okay.

HESTER. But what about the competition?

JASMINE. You *have* come all this way.

BERNIE. I got what I came for.

Beat.

I got to be part of something.

They close in on BERNIE *and hug her. They freeze in the hug*.

Downstage the PRODUCERS *enter*.

They're all talking animatedly at each other. Like a gaggle of geese.

FRANKIE *approaches them*.

FRANKIE. Excuse me?

The PRODUCERS *ignore her*.

Excuse me?

They ignore her.

Oi!

They fall silent.

PRODUCERS. What is it, Frankie?

FRANKIE. I think we have a problem.

She points upstage – where the CONTESTANTS *are embraced in a hug.*

The PRODUCERS *turn to look at them.*

They step closer – moving as they do – as one.

PRODUCERS. For once, Frankie, I think you might be right.

The PRESENTERS *enter.*

The PRODUCERS *exit with* FRANKIE.

11. The Presenters, Again

They speak in stage whispers.

PRESENTER 2. Welcome back, folks.

PRESENTER 1. We're backstage taking an exclusive look at our Bright Young Things.

PRESENTER 2. There's just three rounds to go –

PRESENTER 1. And after front-runner Bernadette's shock exit –

PRESENTER 2. It's anyone's to play for, as we head into:

PRESENTER 1 *and* 2. Round Three. Spelling Bee.

12. Round Three – Spelling

The holding room. As the CONTESTANTS *get into their positions for this scene, the offstage characters are chanting, almost like a mantra. Or a meditation tape.*

VOICES. Anything, everything, anything, everything, anything.

Until SHEARA *breaks the sound with her line –*

SHEARA. I don't know!

She is sat with JASMINE – *who's testing her out of a book.*

JASMINE. Well, you can't say that up there.

SHEARA. I can't think any more.

JASMINE. Guess at least. Go on – 'Schadenfreude'.

SHEARA. I don't even know what it means.

HESTER *is noisily going through her backpack.*

HESTER. Where…

JASMINE (*reading*). Schadenfreude. Pleasure derived by someone from another person's misfortune.

SHEARA. S… C… H… A… D… E… N. F. R. E. U. D.

JASMINE. Uh-uh. There's an 'e' on the end.

SHEARA. Can we take a break?

JASMINE. Narcissist.

HESTER. I could have sworn…

JASMINE. Speaking of which… Hester, do you mind? It's like revising in a wind tunnel with all that huffing and puffing.

HESTER. I had it.

SHEARA. Had what?

HESTER. Nelson's foot. I've looked everywhere.

SHEARA. It can't have gone far.

ROCHELLE. Have you checked your pockets?

HESTER. Of course I have.

ROCHELLE. You know when you look in the same place for something three times and then it ends up being there anyway?

HESTER. It's not in my pockets!

SHEARA. Jas?

JASMINE. How do I know? Anyway we're working.

HESTER. I've looked everywhere.

SHEARA. We'll help. Won't we, Jasmine?

A beat, then JASMINE *gets up to look too.*

Right. Where did you last have it?

HESTER. If I knew that…

ROCHELLE. Think. Take a breath.

HESTER. I'm up next.

JASMINE. You sure this isn't a ploy? Get us all running round after you so we lose concentration?

ROCHELLE. We should all check our pockets. Bags.

HESTER. I can't go on without it.

JASMINE. I thought you didn't believe in luck?

FRANKIE (*from off*). Hester to the stage please, Hester to the stage.

HESTER. Well, that's it then.

ROCHELLE. Try to keep calm. Do something relaxing.

HESTER *starts doing frantic Sun Salutations.*

HESTER. I'm not going up there and humiliating myself. No way.

ROCHELLE. You're not going to humiliate yourself.

HESTER (*still doing yoga*). Of course I am. Do you know how many people hate me?

JASMINE (*under her breath*). I can hazard a guess.

SHEARA. Jasmine!

JASMINE. Right!

SHEARA (*to* JASMINE). Where are you going?

JASMINE. To check the corridors.

JASMINE *exits.*

HESTER. They'd love to see me fail. Have a good laugh at old Hester, the kid who had everything and still couldn't win.

HESTER *is doing some kind of deep breathing, martial arts thing.*

FRANKIE *enters.*

FRANKIE. Hester? You're being called.

SHEARA. She just needs one more minute. To… warm up.

ROCHELLE. She's lost her mascot.

SHEARA. We've looked everywhere.

FRANKIE. You don't think someone might have hidden it?

SHEARA. On purpose?

FRANKIE. I see it all the time. Last year, *Celebrity Ice Capades* – a respected newsreader tied her opponent's bootlaces together.

ROCHELLE. Right.

FRANKIE. Amazing really. The lengths people will go to to win.

Offstage a chant is starting up.

VOICES. Hester, Hester, Hester…

HESTER. What am I going to do?

FRANKIE. Let me see if Neil's got anything up his sleeve.

FRANKIE *exits.*

SHEARA (*to* ROCHELLE). I know Jas comes across a bit… But she'd never do this. Not once she saw how upset Hester is.

HESTER. Never retreat, never surrender. Never retreat…

The PRODUCERS *enter.*

Oh heck.

PRODUCERS. Hester, old thing. How are we?

A little birdy tells us you're feeling a bit overwhelmed.

HESTER. I'm fine. Better than fine.

PRODUCERS. You know you can talk to us?

HESTER. I can?

PRODUCERS. Contestants' welfare is our first priority.

HESTER. It is?

PRODUCERS. Of course.

Now tell us exactly what the problem is.

Beat.

HESTER. I think it's just the pressure.

PRODUCERS. Hester, do you know what coal is made of?

HESTER. Is this one of my questions?

PRODUCERS. Anyone?

ROCHELLE. Carbon, mostly.

PRODUCERS. Right. Now. Do you know what diamonds are made of?

ROCHELLE. Also carbon

PRODUCERS. Correct.

So what's the difference between the two?

ROCHELLE. If I'm remembering right, diamonds are a very pure crystalline –

All the PRODUCERS *look at* ROCHELLE.

PRODUCERS. Shhhhhhh!

The difference, Hester, is pressure.

Carbon, when left to its own devices will become a lump of coal.

But add enough pressure you can make…

HESTER. A diamond?

PRODUCERS. Precisely.

No pressure, no diamonds.

Now it's up to you.

Which do you want to be?

13. The End of the World

In the studio.

NEIL PULLOVER. Why do cats make good lawyers? Because they're very PURR-suasive.

The sound of boos.

PRESENTER 1. Thank you, Neil!

NEIL PULLOVER. I've got more.

HESTER *steps onto the podium.*

PRESENTER 2. Just in time. Hester, welcome back to the podium.

PRESENTER 1. We thought we might have lost you there?

HESTER. No. A Hawthorne never gives up.

PRESENTER 2. There's the Hester we know and love.

PRESENTER 1. So, Lady Regina. It's over to you for the questions.

REGINA RUSTINGTON. Hester. Could you please spell the word…

But we don't hear what the word is. Because in its place is an ALMIGHTY ROAR – like a clap of thunder.

HESTER. I'm sorry, do you mind repeating the question?

REGINA RUSTINGTON. Of course. Your word is…

Again, the sound of thunder. Louder this time. And it's growing. The thunder becomes a storm.

HESTER (*over the noise*). I can't hear you, could you please...

Beat.

(*To herself*). Never surrender, never retreat.

The JUDGES *and* PRESENTERS *join in.*

JUDGES/PRESENTERS. Never surrender, never retreat.

Offstage voices join in. The sound of the storm is still swirling.

VOICES. Never surrender, never retreat.

Flooding and gun shots and earthquakes. It sounds like the end of the world.

HESTER. I SURRENDER!!!!!!

HESTER *covers her head, no one else does.*

Then silence.

PRESENTER 1. Hester?

PRESENTER 2. Unlucky Hester.

HESTER. What happened?

REGINA RUSTINGTON. I'm afraid you failed to answer any of your questions.

HESTER. That's all?

NEIL PULLOVER. Do you understand? You're out the competition.

HESTER. Right. But it's not the end of the world.

Beat.

Is it?

14. Everything's About to Change

ROCHELLE'S DAD *enters*.

ROCHELLE'S DAD. Rochelle?

ROCHELLE. Dad.

ROCHELLE'S DAD. Shouldn't you be revising?

ROCHELLE. Lunch break. What you doing back here?

ROCHELLE'S DAD. If anyone asks there's a leak in the loos. I don't think I'm allowed to talk to contestants. Especially not semi-finalists.

ROCHELLE. It's not the FA Cup.

ROCHELLE'S DAD. No. It's better. This time my team have actually got a chance of winning.

ROCHELLE. I told you, I'm not going to win.

ROCHELLE'S DAD. Everything's about to change, Rochelle, you'll see. I can feel it.

15. Got You

A corridor. SHEARA *is alone, looking at a book.*

JASMINE *enters holding two brown bags.*

JASMINE. There you are. Why are you skulking in a corridor?

SHEARA. I just wanted a minute on my own.

JASMINE. Two words. You're welcome.

> JASMINE *hands her a brown paper bag.*

> I had to beat Rochelle to the last cheese one so we could have the same.

> SHEARA *takes the bag.*

> You're right, it's nice to be alone.

SHEARA. Jas, don't you ever get tired?

JASMINE. Told you we should have got to bed earlier.

SHEARA. No, I mean tired of this. Competing.

JASMINE. It's only one day.

SHEARA. It's *every* minute of every day.

JASMINE. What are you –

SHEARA. Why are you better at everything than me?

Beat.

JASMINE. I'm not.

SHEARA. First to walk. First to ride your bike.

JASMINE. You're talking rubbish.

SHEARA. We're meant to be the same.

JASMINE. We are. You just need more confidence. Don't worry so much about other people.

SHEARA. You mean don't make friends.

JASMINE. Friends like Rochelle?

SHEARA. She's nice.

JASMINE. She's obviously clever.

SHEARA. So?

JASMINE. So it's a bit suspicious, isn't it? How she just happened to be here at the right moment.

SHEARA. You just think everyone wants to win as badly as you do.

JASMINE. They do! Anyone who says different is lying.

SHEARA. That's not true.

JASMINE. You're honestly telling me, that you don't want this more than anything else in your entire life?

Beat.

SHEARA *picks the book up again*.

SHEARA. Come on then.

JASMINE. What…

SHEARA. I'll test you.

JASMINE. I meant what I said earlier, you know, about not being here to make friends. I don't need anyone else. Not when I've got you.

16. Round Four – General Knowledge

PRESENTER 1. So here we are.

PRESENTER 2. The penultimate round, and our competitors' last shot at the final.

PRESENTER 1. With Jasmine scoring a fantastic five points in this round, she's guaranteed her place in the live final.

PRESENTER 2. Sister Sheara has scored a respectable three, but with Rochelle still to play who will go through to the live final?

PRESENTER 1. There's only one way to find out.

PRESENTER 2. Let's welcome Rochelle to the podium to play:

PRESENTERS 1 *and* 2. Round Four. General Knowledge.

VOICES. Anything, everything, anything, everything, anything.

ROCHELLE *steps up on the podium*.

REGINA RUSTINGTON. Welcome back, Rochelle. You must score a minimum of four points to give you a chance at the final. There can be no passes in this round. You have one minute to answer as many questions as you can. Do you understand?

ROCHELLE. Yes.

REGINA RUSTINGTON. Then we'll begin. Which musical features songs by Freddie Mercury and the rock band Queen?

ROCHELLE. *We Will Rock You*?

The ding of a triangle.

REGINA RUSTINGTON. Correct.

NEIL PULLOVER. Which oxidising agent is commonly found
in cleaning fluids?

ROCHELLE. Sodium percarbonate.

Ding.

NEIL PULLOVER. Which appendage did Horatio Nelson
famously lose?

ROCHELLE. His right arm?

Ding.

REGINA RUSTINGTON. Which household object was
invented by Thomas Edison?

ROCHELLE. Erm…

REGINA RUSTINGTON. Would you like me to repeat the
question?

The sound of rain.

ROCHELLE *looks up.*

A woman walks on stage. She's got a suitcase. This is
ROCHELLE'S MUM.

REGINA RUSTINGTON. I said would you like me to repeat
the question?

(*Or, if* REGINA RUSTINGTON *is played by the same actor
as* ROCHELLE'S MUM, *she transforms in front of us – other
actors bring on a suitcase and coat and dress her on stage.*)

She should have her back to ROCHELLE *by now.*

ROCHELLE. Mum?

One scene bleeds into another.

ROCHELLE'S MUM *turns around, like she's just been
caught.*

ROCHELLE'S MUM. Rochelle.

Beat.

You're back early.

ROCHELLE. Athletics was cancelled. The rain. Did they call?

ROCHELLE'S MUM. What?

ROCHELLE. The school.

ROCHELLE'S MUM. Oh. No.

ROCHELLE. You're sure?

ROCHELLE'S MUM. I'm sure, love.

ROCHELLE. What d'you think it means?

ROCHELLE MUM. Just that they haven't decided yet.

ROCHELLE. Yeah. I s'pose. What's for dinner?

ROCHELLE'S MUM. There's something on the side.

ROCHELLE. You going somewhere?

ROCHELLE'S MUM. Rochelle, I...

The phone rings. Loud.

ROCHELLE. That's them. D'you think it's them?

ROCHELLE'S MUM. Go on then.

ROCHELLE *exits.* ROCHELLE'S MUM *is left alone onstage.
She lingers a moment. Then picks up her bag and exits.*

ROCHELLE (*off*). You're not gonna believe it, Mum...

ROCHELLE *re-enters.*

The sound of the door closing.

Beat.

Mum?

The woman is gone. We're back in the studio.

REGINA RUSTINGTON. Rochelle, we're going to have to
push you for an answer.

ROCHELLE. The phone. He invented the phone.

A sound – Uh-uh.

REGINA RUSTINGTON. Sorry, Rochelle. The correct answer is the lightbulb.

ROCHELLE. But… no, I'm sure…

REGINA RUSTINGTON. Congratulations on getting this far.

ROCHELLE. Please. Please can I have another question?

REGINA RUSTINGTON. I'm sorry, Rochelle.

ROCHELLE. But this is my only chance.

Beat.

So that's it? It can't be…

REGINA RUSTINGTON. It is. It's over, Rochelle.

17. The Jacket

SHEARA *is in the holding room.*

SHEARA. **The day we were born, I was first out. People are always surprised when they hear that. I think a lot about what it must be like to be Jasmine. How close I was to being her. Just like me, only… better.**

ROCHELLE *enters.*

ROCHELLE. Hey.

SHEARA. Hey.

ROCHELLE. Congratulations.

SHEARA. Oh. Yeah. Thanks.

ROCHELLE. Just came to collect my stuff.

SHEARA. Sorry you didn't get to the final.

ROCHELLE. It's fine.

SHEARA. I didn't realise you wanted to. I mean, you never seemed bothered.

ROCHELLE. I don't think I realised either.

Beat.

Where's Jasmine?

SHEARA. Bathroom. Even she draws the line at joint toilet breaks.

ROCHELLE. It must be nice. Having someone to share everything with. Like you must never get lonely.

SHEARA. You know, my mum's got this picture of us. From when she was pregnant. She said every time they did a scan, me and Jas had our heads pressed up against each other, like we were whispering secrets. Our little hands gripping together tight. I always thought I knew everything about her. But now… I dunno.

Beat.

I've never been on my own. It's different to never being lonely.

ROCHELLE. Yeah.

SHEARA. I think she took Hester's mascot. Jasmine, I mean. I think it was her.

ROCHELLE. You're sure?

Beat.

SHEARA. It was nice to meet you.

ROCHELLE. Good luck, Sheara.

SHEARA. Thanks. I think I'm going to need it.

ROCHELLE *exits.*

SHEARA *picks up* ROCHELLE*'s jacket.*

SHEARA. Here, you forgot this.

But ROCHELLE*'s already gone.*

She holds it up against herself.

Loud music plays – something punky, rebellious. Or if you've got a proper drum kit, get someone rolling on that!

SHEARA *puts on the jacket, changes her hairstyle so it's messy. She could make a rip in her tights or tie a scarf round her head. Other actors can come onstage to help with this and add items if it helps.*

The important thing for the story is that by the end of this sequence she doesn't match with JASMINE *any more.*

18. We Did It

JASMINE *enters and the music stops.*

JASMINE. What are you doing?

Beat.

Is that Rochelle's jacket?

SHEARA. Should I have asked your permission?

JASMINE. Never mind. None of that matters now. We made it, Shear. The final.

Beat.

I thought you'd be happy?

SHEARA. Did you take it?

JASMINE. What?

SHEARA. Hester's mascot. Nelson's foot. Did you take it?

JASMINE. No. Why?

SHEARA. You made it clear you didn't like Hester.

JASMINE. I'm not a thief.

SHEARA. I was so sure. I told everyone you wouldn't do something like that.

JASMINE. Did Rochelle put this in your head?

SHEARA. You said it yourself. You want this more than anything else in the entire world.

JASMINE. I wanted both of us to get to the final.

SHEARA. Why?

JASMINE. Because...

SHEARA. Because you knew you could beat me?

JASMINE. No! The opposite.

Beat.

I'm going to let you win.

Beat.

I want you to get the trophy. You're always so hard on yourself. And you don't see how brilliant you are. You've been pulling away from me for months, Shear. I can't stand it. I just want everything to be how it was.

Beat.

SHEARA. *Let* me win?

JASMINE. I didn't mean...

FRANKIE *enters.*

FRANKIE. So. Is everybody ready?

19. Bus Stop

ROCHELLE *and her* DAD *wait at the bus stop.*

ROCHELLE'S DAD. No sign of this bus.

Beat.

Feel like I've been waiting forever.

Beat.

We can go back if you want? Watch the final with the others.

ROCHELLE. Nah, I'm good.

ROCHELLE'S DAD. Don't be too down in the dumps. You did great. You never know, maybe there'll be a message on the machine when we get in?

Beat.

Dunno where this bus is.

Beat.

He rubs his hands together for the cold.

Puts them in his pocket.

Here.

He hands her something.

I meant to give it to you earlier. Found it when I was cleaning up. Supposed to be lucky, aren't they? Funny thing to come across. A rabbit's foot.

ROCHELLE. Dad. Where did you find this?

The PRESENTERS enter as ROCHELLE and her DAD exit.

20. Head-to-Head

PRESENTER 1. Welcome back.

PRESENTER 2. We're coming to you live from the studio.

PRESENTER 1. We're just one round away from crowning this year's Bright Young Thing, but first let's give a warm welcome back to our contestants:

PRESENTER 2. Amber,

PRESENTER 1. Hester,

PRESENTER 2. Bernadette,

PRESENTER 1. And this year's finalists – THE TWINS!

Down the sides, offstage actors are no longer 'offstage'.
They become the live audience, along with the
CONTESTANTS. *They all applaud as the* TWINS *step onto*
the front two blocks. Two podiums.

PRESENTER 2. Well done to every single one of you. Even
those that didn't stick around, not mentioning any names –

PRESENTER 1. Rochelle.

PRESENTER 2. Jasmine. How does it feel to get to the final? Is
it everything you imagined.

JASMINE. Honestly? No.

The PRODUCERS *stand. They shake their heads.*

PRODUCERS. Autocue. Read the autocue.

JASMINE (*faking it*). It's… It's even better.

The PRODUCERS *give her a thumbs-up.*

PRESENTER 1. Now Sheara, you won the coin toss backstage,
so you choose who gets the first question.

SHEARA. Me. I'll go first.

Here's where we hand back over to you, the cast.

The challenge here is to physically tell the story that each
twin is asked three questions in turn, all of which are
answered correctly.

But when JASMINE *is asked her fourth question – she gets*
it wrong.

I've written a suggestion below of how to stage this. But you
might have other ideas. And if you do, that's just great.

Set to music:

The CROWD *– made up of all the other actors – goes back*
and forward between the TWINS *as if they're watching a*
tennis match.

Each time a question is correctly answered, a triangle dings
– or whatever you've established as your 'correct' sound
earlier in the show.

Until JASMINE*'s fourth question when a horn – or again whatever you've established as your 'incorrect' noise – sounds.*

REGINA RUSTINGTON. I'm sorry, Jasmine. That was an incorrect answer.

The CROWD *gasps.*

PRESENTER 1. Now if Sheara scores this next point, she'll take home the trophy.

REGINA RUSTINGTON. Sheara. For this year's title –

Dramatic pause.

Which word, of German origin, has the meaning 'pleasure derived from someone else's misfortune'?

SHEARA. I know this.

NEIL PULLOVER. You do?

REGINA RUSTINGTON. Well then, Sheara?

SHEARA. The answer is…

ROCHELLE (*offstage*). Wait!

The CROWD *gasps again.*

SHEARA. Rochelle?

PRODUCERS. I thought she'd gone?

She's blocking Camera Two.

PRESENTER 1. Rochelle. Welcome back.

ROCHELLE. I wanted to talk to Sheara.

PRESENTER 2. We're live on air, Rochelle, could it wait?

ROCHELLE. I'm actually quite sick of waiting.

JASMINE. What's she talking about?

ROCHELLE. This!

ROCHELLE *holds something up. The rabbit's foot.*

HESTER. Nelson's foot!

JASMINE. You had it all this time?

ROCHELLE. No.

JASMINE. I knew it.

ROCHELLE. You don't understand.

JASMINE. You made Sheara think I stole it.

ROCHELLE. No.

JASMINE. You gave her your jacket.

SHEARA. I took it. And I'm allowed to wear what I want.

ROCHELLE. Dad. Tell them.

ROCHELLE'S DAD. Tell them what?

ROCHELLE. Where you found it.

ROCHELLE'S DAD. I don't know, Rochelle, the bosses are just there.

ROCHELLE. You can do it.

ROCHELLE'S DAD *steps forward.*

He clears his throat.

ROCHELLE'S DAD. I was cleaning the producers' office. And I found it.

Beat.

In the wastepaper basket.

Beat.

Which is, quite frankly, irresponsible. It should have at least gone in the food bin.

ROCHELLE. Thanks, Dad.

HESTER. You stole it?

HESTER *points at the* PRODUCERS.

Two of them speak at the same time:

PRODUCERS. No. / Yes.

Beat.

We were going to give it back.

HESTER. It was in the bin.

ROCHELLE'S DAD. In the incorrect bin at that!

ROCHELLE. We've got it, Dad.

HESTER. Why?

PRODUCERS. Can we talk about this later?

We've got a competition to finish and a winner to crown.

Two competitive sisters go head-to-head in a gruelling battle –

SHEARA. You want us to hate each other?

PRODUCERS. She's admitting it. She hates her sister.

She's ravaged by jealousy.

ROCHELLE. You can't keep putting words in our mouths. We're not puppets or 'things'. We've got our own voices. And we're telling our own stories.

The CROWD *cheers.*

From her seat in the crowd, BERNIE *stands.*

BERNIE. I'm Bernadette. And nobody in my whole life has ever called me The Brain.

AMBER *stands.*

AMBER. I'm Amber. I stole my nan's biscuits. And I'm not even sorry.

HESTER *stands.*

HESTER. I'm not as confident as I pretend to be.

REGINA RUSTINGTON *stands.*

REGINA RUSTINGTON. I'm more scared of children than they are of me.

NEIL PULLOVER *stands.*

NEIL PULLOVER. I'm Neil and I don't think cats are funny!

Beat.

JASMINE. I don't get it.

PRODUCERS. You're supposed to be bright.

JASMINE. We worked so hard to get here. And you wanted to ruin it?

PRODUCERS. 'Worked hard'? Please. You don't actually think you're the cleverest child in the whole country? I mean how would you even calculate that?

JASMINE. But… all the tests.

PRODUCERS. Screen tests. Personality tests.

Sure, there's a basic standard but mostly it's a casting process.

They point to SHEARA.

Loser.

They point to BERNIE.

Geek.

They point to JASMINE.

Villain.

They point to AMBER.

Freak.

The CROWD *gasps*.

Oh don't give me all that.

You're the ones watching.

The CROWD *boos the* PRODUCERS.

We had high hopes for you, Rochelle. Your dad had told us all about you. We thought we'd found the perfect person for the part.

ROCHELLE. What part?

Beat.

JASMINE. The underdog.

PRODUCERS. Very good, Jasmine.

ROCHELLE. Underdog?

JASMINE. They set you up, Rochelle. They set us all up.

PRODUCERS. Not a set-up. But a story.

Would you tune in to watch one of this lot win?

They gesture the other CONTESTANTS.

Of course not.

Too obvious. Too *easy*.

But the cleaner's daughter...

ROCHELLE'S DAD. So, none of this is real?

PRODUCERS. People don't want real – they want something
far better. They want hope.

We're not the bad guys. If anything, we're heroes.

BERNIE. I really doubt that.

PRODUCERS. We give people something to hold out for.

A belief that one moment you can be going about your
boring, ordinary, little life and the next – the phone rings.
And everything changes.

Sounds good, doesn't it, Sheara?

The PRODUCERS *crowd around* SHEARA.

Sheara, if you answer this question you could take home
the prize.

Don't think your sister wouldn't, if the shoe was on the
other foot.

Aren't you sick of living in her shadow?

This is your one chance to take her on, head-to-head.

SHEARA. We've spent our whole lives head-to-head.

JASMINE. That's not true!

SHEARA (*gentle*). Of course it is. Head-to-head.

Beat.

Toe-to-toe.

Beat.

Hand-to-hand.

She steps down off the podium and holds out a hand for
JASMINE *to do the same.*

JASMINE. I wasn't pretending. I really got it wrong.

SHEARA. I know.

JASMINE. You could have beaten me.

SHEARA. I never needed to beat you at something, Jas. I just
need a bit of space. And maybe to pick my own lunch every
now and again.

JASMINE. I think I can manage that.

ROCHELLE. Here, Hester.

ROCHELLE *hands* HESTER *back Nelson's foot.*

HESTER. You know what? I don't think I need this any more.

PRODUCERS. Now girls, come back.

We've got a show to make.

We're under a lot of pressure.

Though you know what they say about pressure?

ROCHELLE. You know it's actually a myth that you can make
diamonds out of coal?

PRODUCERS. It is?

BERNIE. Oh yes. It's a very specific set of circumstances that
have to come together to produce a diamond.

PRODUCERS. But... but...

JASMINE. Come on. We'll explain it to you.

The stage clears.

ROCHELLE *is about to leave when –*

FRANKIE. Rochelle? You forgot this.

ROCHELLE. What?

FRANKIE. Sheara and Jasmine both forfeited their places. The rules say there has to be a winner. So...

She hands ROCHELLE *the cup – The Golden Brain.*

Congratulations.

FRANKIE *exits.*

ROCHELLE *holds the cup in her hands.*

She sets it down on one of the blocks.

Then she sets the phone from the first scene next to it.

She stares at the phone a moment.

21. A Phone Rings

ROCHELLE'S DAD (*offstage*). Roch?

He enters.

I was calling you.

ROCHELLE. Sorry.

ROCHELLE'S DAD. Look at that, eh.

ROCHELLE. I didn't win. Not really.

Beat.

Do you think... do you think she was watching?

ROCHELLE'S DAD. I don't know, love.

ROCHELLE. I thought she might call.

ROCHELLE'S DAD. You know, you *did* win. I'm not talking about some poxy cup. You took your story in your hands and you owned it. But nothing you did today was gonna make her come home. Just like nothing you did made her go.

Beat.

So. Come Monday we're gonna call that school, see if there's still a place –

ROCHELLE. Dad.

ROCHELLE'S DAD. I'll be alright without you, you know. If it's what you want?

ROCHELLE. It is.

ROCHELLE'S DAD. Good. That's settled then. And in the meantime I owe you a trip. So what's it to be? Cinema? Museum? If we hurry we can catch the last of that paint drying next door.

ROCHELLE. Erm… Cinema.

Do you remember the moment just before your life changed?

ROCHELLE'S DAD. You check the listings, I'll get the car warmed up.

ROCHELLE. **A door opens.**

ROCHELLE'S DAD (*leaving the house*). You coming?

ROCHELLE. **A storm breaks.**

The phone on the table rings. They both look at it.

It rings and rings.

ROCHELLE'S DAD. I'll see you out there.

ROCHELLE'S DAD *exits, leaving the phone ringing on stage.*

A beat.

Then ROCHELLE *follows.*

End.